1 MONTH OF
FREE
READING

at

www.ForgottenBooks.com

By purchasing this book you are eligible for one month membership to ForgottenBooks.com, giving you unlimited access to our entire collection of over 1,000,000 titles via our web site and mobile apps.

To claim your free month visit: www.forgottenbooks.com/free317909

ISBN 978-0-332-43137-6
PIBN 10317909

A York Pioneer's Recollections

CANADA OUR HOME

—OF A—

Visit to "The Emerald Isle,"

AND HIS NATIVE TOWN,

AFTER AN ABSENCE OF FORTY YEARS,

TOGETHER WITH AMUSING INCIDENTS, AND ANECDOTES OF PLACES
AND ODD CHARACTERS MET WITH, IN IRELAND AND
OTHER PARTS OF THE BRITISH ISLES.

BY E. M. MORPHY,

*Author of "'Sainty' Smith; or, The School Upon the Hill," and "Youthful
Days in Erin and Canada."*

Principal Loudon

With the Author's Compliments

E. M. MORPHY, SON & CO.

Diamond Merchants and Jewellers,

141 YONGE STREET, TORONTO.

GOLD WATCHES.

Ladies' Gold Watches, *Swiss*, $10, $15, $20, $25.
" " " *American*, $25, $30, $40, $50, $60.
Gents' " . " " $30, $40, $50 to $100.
" " " " and *Swiss* Chrono-
graphs, Minute and Quarter Repeaters, $75, $100
to $250.
Gents' Filled Gold Watches, $20, $25. $30.
Ladies' " " " $15, $20, $25.

SILVER AND NICKLE WATCHES.

Ladies' Nickle Watches, $3 to $4.
" Silver " $5, $6, $8, $10.
Boys' Nickle " $2.50, $3, $4.50.
" Silver " $6, $8, $10.
Gents' " " $8, $10, $12, $15 to $30.

GOLD CHAINS.

Gents' Gold Alberts, $8, $10, $15, $20, $25, $30.
Ladies' " " $8, $9.50, $12, $15, $18, $20.
" " Guards, $12, $15, $18, $20, $25, $30.
" " Fobs, $7.50, $9.50, $12, $15, $18, $20.
" " Necklets, $10, $15, $18, $25, $30.

GOLD RINGS.

Wedding Rings, $3, $5, $8, $10.
Band Rings, $2.50, $3.50, $4.50, $6, $8.
Chased Rings, $3, $4.50, $6, $8, $10.
Gem Rings, Garnet and Pearls, $2, $2.50, $4, $5, $6.
Gem Rings, Rubies and Pearls, $4.50, $6, $8, $10, $12.
Gem Rings (*Engagement*) Diamonds, $10, $12, $15,
$20, $30.
Gents' Signet Rings, $3, $5, $8, $12.

GOLD LOCKETS AND CHARMS.

Ladies' Gold Lockets, $4, $6, $7, $9, $10, $12, $14.
Gents' Gold Lockets, $6, $8, $10.
Gents' Gold Seals, $4.50, $6, $8.50, $10.

GOLD BRACELETS.

Gold Bangles, $5, $6, $10, $15.
Band Bracelets, $8, $10, $15, $25.
Band Bracelets, set with Rubies and Pearls, $15, $18,
$25.

GOLD BROOCHES AND EAR-
RINGS.

Gold Brooches, $4, $6, $10, $14, $18, $20.
Gold Bar Pins, $3, $5, $7.50, $10, $15.
Gold Earrings, $1.50, $2.50, $4, $5.50, $8.

GOLD SETS.

Ten Carat Gold Sets, $8, $9.50, $12, $14, $15.
Fifteen Carat Gold Sets. $15, $20, $24, $30, $35.

DIAMONDS.

Diamond Rings, $10, $15, $20, $25, $35, $50.
Diamond Earrings, $7.50, $12, $20, $35, $50.
Diamond Bar Pins, $12, $16.50, $20, $25.
Diamond Scarf Pins, $8.50, $15, $25, $40, $50.
Diamond Studs, $10, $14, $17.50, $20, $25.
Diamond Collar Buttons, $10, $15, $20, $25, $30.

GOLD SCARF PINS.

New Patterns, $1, $1.50, $2, $3.50, $5.
Diamond, $8.50, $12, $15, $20.

GOLD BUTTONS.

Gents' Gold Cuff Buttons, $3, $4, $5, $6, $8, $10.
Ladies' Gold Cuff Buttons, $3, $4, $6.
Gold Cuff Links, $4, $5, $7.50, $10.
Ladies' Gold Collar Buttons, $1.25, $1.50, $2, $3.
Gents' Gold Collar Buttons, $1.50, $2, $3.
Gents' Gold Shirt Studs, per set, $2, $3, $5.

ROLLED GOLD JEWELLERY.

Gents' Alberts, $2.50, $3.50, $5, $6, $7.50.
Ladies' Alberts, $2, $2.50, $3, $5, $6.50.
Ladies' Fobs, $2, $2.50, $3, $5.
Rolled Gold Brooches, $1, $1.50, $2.50.
Rolled Gold Bar Pins, 75c., $1, $1.50.
Rolled Gold Earrings, 50c., 75c., $1.
Rolled Gold Necklets, $2.50, $3.50, $5, $6.
Rolled Gold Lockets, $1, $2, $3.
Rolled Gold Cuff Buttons, 50c., 75c., $1, $1.50, $2.
Rolled Gold Collar Buttons, 25c., 50c.
Rolled Gold Bracelets, 75c., $1.50, $3, $5.
Rolled Gold Scarf Pins, 50c., 75c., $1.

SILVER JEWELLERY.

Silver Brooches, 50c., 75c., $1, $1.50, $2.
Silver Earrings, 25c., 50c., 60c., 75c., $1.
Silver Necklets, $1.50, $2, $3.50, $5.
Silver Lockets, $1.50, $2, $3.50, $5.
Silver Bangle Bracelets, 50c., 75c., $1, $2, $3.
Silver Band Bracelets, $1.50, $2.50, $4.
Ladies' Silver Fobs, $1, $1.50, $2, $2.50.
Gents' Silver Alberts, $2, $3, $5.
Ladies' Silver Cuff Buttons, 75c., $1.
Gents' Silver Cuff Buttons, $1, $1.50, $2.
Silver Collar Buttons, 25c., 50c., 75c.
Silver Cuff Links, $1, $1.25, $1.75.
Silver Thimbles, 25c., 50c., 75c.

☞ Price List continued on third page of cover.

A Re-Visit to the Emerald Isle.

CHAPTER I.

" Far westward lies an isle of ancient fame,
　By nature blessed, and Ireland is her name;
　Enrolled in books, exhaustless in her store
　Of vein silver, and of golden ore;
　Her fruitful soil forever teems with wealth,
　With genial waters, and her air with health.
　Her verdant fields with 'milk and honey flow,'
　Her woolly fleeces vie with virgin snow;
　Her waving furrows float with bearded corn,
　And arms and arts her envious sons adorn.
　No savage bear with lawless fury roves,
　No roaring lion through her peaceful groves;
　No poison here infects, no scaly snakes
　Creep through her grass, nor toad among her lakes.
　An island worthy of its pious race,
　In war triumphant, and unmatched in peace." *

AFTER spending many years in Canada, the writer had a great desire to re-visit "the old sod" and the scenes of his childhood. At length the time arrived when that wish was to be gratified. In the spring of 1876, several members of his family, consisting of two brothers, a brother-in-law, a nephew and a cousin, made arrangements for a tour of Europe, including the British Isles. The writer joined the party, and was another "spoke in the wheel."

We embarked on one of the Allan steamers at Quebec, and had a pleasant passage of ten days. I will not detain the reader with the description of a sea voyage, which has been so often and well described, further than to say that our fellow-passengers were cosmopolitan, with whom we soon became familiar, and spent most of our time in the smoking-room, hearing and telling *yarns,* also in the spacious saloon, especially at the dinner table, where many of the guests indulged in *something stronger than water,* but not all, as we had several total abstainers, who joined the writer in the frequent discussions we had on the temperance question—our party flattering themselves that they always had the best of the argument.

We had been nine days sailing, and expected to see land very soon. On the morning of the tenth day we were awakened by the sound of the steward's bell and his peculiar English accent, calling out

* This poem is supposed to have been written over a thousand years ago, when Ireland was called "The Island of Saints."

"HIRELAND! HIRELAND! IN VIEW!"

We made a hasty toilet and rushed on deck, where we were soon joined by others with telescopes and opera glasses, gazing at a little speck in the dim distance. Just then we were amused at an enthusiastic countryman of ours who, on getting his first view of "the dear little isle of the ocean," threw up his cap, crowed like a rooster, and, in a manly and musical voice, sang the following patriotic lines:

> "If England were my place of birth, I'd love her tranquil shore,
> If bonny Scotland were my home, her mountains I'd adore ;
> For pleasant days in both I've spent, I ne'er again shall roam,
> Then steer my barque to Erin's Isle, for Erin is my home.

> CHORUS—"Then steer my barque," etc.

The enthusiasm was infectious, as all the Irish passengers joined in the refrain.

After breakfast, a number of the saloon passengers sat on deck looking toward the little island in the distance, which appeared to be increasing in size as we approached it. The conversation was, IRELAND AND ITS EVENTFUL HISTORY. How the amalgamation, or fusion, of the Celt, Dane, Saxon, Norman, Scot, Hanoverian, Huguenot, Palatine and others, had produced a type of manhood, possessing many of the traits of the races from which they had descended, especially the Danes, in their roving tendency, as IRISHMEN ARE TO BE FOUND IN EVERY PART OF THE GLOBE—governors, statesmen, warriors, and in the learned professions, in which they excel; also among the hardy sons of toil, clearing forests, digging canals and on railroads, building gaols and often *occupying them*, through indiscretion in overheating the Celtic blood with STRONG DRINK, THE CURSE OF EVERY COUNTRY, as well as of Ireland.

We were now coming close to land, and were met by a flock of sea gulls, who gave us a cheer of Irish welcome.

From the deck of our vessel we had a view of the white spray dashing against the rock-bound coast, also the mountain peaks looming up in the distance; then came the panoramic scene of old castles, white cottages, green fields, hawthorn hedges and "daisy-clad hills."

Our reverie was interrupted by the boom of a cannon from each side of the vessel, announcing our arrival in Lough Foyle, County Derry.

Here we separated from our party, as the writer had some business to transact in England, afterwards we were to join some of our friends in Ireland.

CHAPTER II.

ENGLAND.

"'There's a land that bears a well-known name,
  Though it is but a little spot ;
We say 'tis the first on the scroll of fame,
  And who shall say it is not ?
Of the deathless ones that shine and live
  In arms, in arts and song,
The brightest the whole wide world can give,
  To that little land belong. '

AFTER passing the Channel Islands, and while approaching "the white cliffs of Old Albion," we stood upon the deck of our steamer and had our first view of

"THE LAND OF THE BRAVE AND THE FREE."

We have already spoken of Ireland and some of the grand men she has given to the world, but we must not be discriminatory in our remarks, as England and Scotland have added their quota of similar characters, making a grand total or galaxy of "burning and shining lights," who have shed their lustre over every part of the civilized world, hence, we in Canada are proud of our connection with Great Britain, and honor the viceroy she sends us as a connecting link.

But a truce to loyalty, and a return to our narrative.

On landing in Liverpool, we were struck with its substantial cut-stone docks, and its miles of shipping. We proceeded to our hotel, and after dinner prepared for a stroll, when the following amusing incident occurred : At the main entrance sat an old pensioner in uniform, with his blue coat ornamented with medals ; he was a guide, and we engaged his services to pilot us through the city.

He described, in glowing language, all the public squares and buildings, and especially Nelson's monument, with its group of allegorical figures, which is a magnificent work of art.

At length he stopped opposite a large gin palace, and said, "Now, sir, if you want a glass of ale, this is one of the best places in Liverpool for '*the genuine stuff.*'" We told him we were not thirsty, and did not require any ; he reluctantly passed on. In a little time he came to a similar house, and stopped again, saying, "If you are not dry, I am, sir." We told him we were total abstainers and did not patronize such places, and how much better it would be if he were so, as DRINKING SPIRITUOUS LIQUORS CREATED AN UNNATURAL THIRST. He replied, "That it was all very well for foreigners to talk

so, but he was *an Hinglishman*, and must have his beer."
Having seen much of the city, we discharged our thirsty guide
by "a tip," and followed him with our eyes till he entered a
low tavern near the docks, and mingled with a lot of common-
looking men and women, who-were smoking long pipes, and
sipping their *yal.*

We understand that a very great change has taken place
since then, as the drinking dens along the docks, where sailors
and others spent their hard earnings, have given place to
COFFEE HOUSES ERECTED BY THE TEMPERANCE FRIENDS OF
LIVERPOOL.

On the following morning we proceeded to the Lime Street
station (as large as a little town), and took passage to Birmingham, where we arrived in about three hours, passing through a
level and highly cultivated pasture land, studded with clumps
of shade trees, under which fat cattle and sheep rested. Then
through the "Black Country," so called, as the smoke of the
iron-smelting furnaces give a grim appearance to everything,
not excepting the workmen, who are as black as genuine
Africans.

Birmingham, the Workshop of the World,

was our destination, and here we soon mixed up among the
manufacturing jewellers, climbing up narrow stairways to little
rooms of branch workmen. And now for another little incident
illustrative of the English artizan.

One day we knocked at the closed door of one of those little
factories. After waiting for some time, the door was opened
by an angry looking woman, who demanded what we wanted.
"To see the jeweller," we replied. "He caunt be seen."
"Why?" "He's at dinner." "How long will I have to wait?"
"An hour and an a'ff."

Hence I discovered that from one to half-past two was the
working-man's dinner time, which was followed by his long
pipe and mug of ale, and to interrupt him was like disturbing
"a dog at a bone." It is proverbial that an Englishman is
fond of a good dinner, and plenty of time for digestion. The
question is, Does the tobacco and ale assist? Total abstainers
answer, No!

CHAPTER III.

LETTERS FROM IRELAND.

WHILE in this busy metropolis we received letters from our
party in Ireland, especially from our brother J., who was the
principal correspondent, a synopsis of one we reproduce:

"After parting with you at Lough Foyle, we spent a day in
the old historic city of Londonderry, a place of so many inter-

esting associations. Our next visit was to Enniskillen and its surroundings, including Ely Lodge, Florence Court, Castle Cool, Necarn Castle, and many other places of interest around Lough Erne and its beautiful islands.

Monaghan, Our Native Town,

was our next stopping place. Here we made a good long stay, visiting scenes of our boyhood, including the extensive and picturesque Rossmore Park, also the fine old castles of Castle Shane, Besmount, Glasslough, Caledon, Raconnell, Cornacassa, etc. We attended divine service in the old parish church and Methodist preaching house. During our visit A PUBLIC DINNER WAS TENDERED TO THE WRITER, as an acknowledgment of kind attention (as they termed it) shown to our townsmen on their arrival in Canada. In the absence of Lord Rossmore, Colonel Lloyd presided over the banquet, which was attended by all the leading merchants and professional men of the town. We also had the honor of lunching with the Lady Dowager of Rossmore Castle. We propose to leave here to-morrow for Dublin, and will write you from there."

I was now anxious to join the party, and hurried up matters, especially as I had some more business to transact in London before recrossing the channel. But I must not omit to mention a very interesting visit and fashionable dinner party I attended while in Birmingham.

On a Saturday afternoon, Mr. G., our agent, who was a thorough business man, a manufacturer, a magistrate and

A CHRISTIAN GENTLEMAN,

invited the writer to spend Sunday with him at his beautiful ivy-covered mansion, some eight miles from the city. Here we were introduced to his highly-cultured family, together with the rector and curate of the parish, and many other distinguished guests.

The dinner was a fashionable one, and here my temperance principles were put to the test when the champagne and other liquors were placed before me. To "the pleasure of wine" I begged to be excused, but would join "in ADAM'S ALE." At this juncture the young curate addressed me as follows: "Are you a total abstainer Mr. M. ?" "Yes, sir." "I am very glad to find I am not alone at Mr. G.'s table," said he. "I am equally pleased to find a brother teetotaler," said the writer.

The dinner lasted about three hours, during which time we had to answer many questions about Canada, which we pictured in the highest colors.

After we had spent some time with the ladies in the drawing-room, the guests (except the writer) withdrew; then a bell pull was touched, and the servants, consisting of about seven, came marching into the dining room and occupied one part of the chamber, the family on the other side. Then Mr. G., like one of the patriarchs of old, with his white flowing locks and beard, conducted family worship in a most earnest and reverent manner. At the close of the service the servants retired in the same order in which they entered; then came the parting scene for the night, parents and children embracing each other in the most affectionate manner, with "Good night, my love, God bless you," etc.

The following day, being Sunday, was spent as the Sabbath day should be kept—not a word on business was spoken. Church in the forenoon, then a cold dinner (as servants were not required to work, but to attend divine service). Our principal topic was missions and Sabbath-schools. We sauntered through lawn and woodland, listening to the songsters of the grove while they warbled forth their notes of praise to the Great Creator.

We shall never forget that delightful visit, which revealed to us that true piety is not confined to any particular denomination, nor to the humble walks of life, but has an extra lustre when found among cultured and refined society. The only thing we did not admire in Mr. G.'s delightful home was the prevailing custom of the English gentry, namely, the wine cup, which, we are happy to know, is being discarded, especially by professing Christians.

CHAPTER IV.

LONDON.

BEFORE leaving Birmingham we were agreeably surprised by the arrival of our brother-in-law A. W. and our other relative G. W., who had separated from the party for a time that they might have a long visit in London. In a little time the tourists were rolling along at the rate of fifty miles an hour.

As we approached the greatest city in the world we asked our brother-in-law, who had lived in London, a few questions about the place: "What's the size of it?" "About 120 square miles." "Population?" "Five millions;" more inhabitants than all of Canada, with its area of more than three and one-half millions of square miles. With this thought in mind, and a curiosity to see the great metropolis, we whirled into Euston station; from thence we proceeded to our hotel in Cheapside. After the evening meal we sauntered out for a stroll to see a part of the city by gas-light. Our walk was along Cheapside to St. Paul's Square, and here we had our first view of

St. Paul's Cathedral by Moonlight.

Its great size, magnificent. columns, and lofty dome fully came up to our expectation.

From here we descended towards the Thames, and soon found ourselves on the famous London Bridge, one of the greatest thoroughfares in the city. As we stood on the centre of this historic spot and looked towards Westminster, the various bridges were outlined with gas lamps; also the Thames Embankment, together with the Houses of Parliament, with the grand Victoria and Clock towers looming up in the distance.

Then turning around, we had a view of the grim old Tower, with its massive turrets and "Traitors' Gate." In the distance were the famous London docks, with their woods of shipping, while the river below us was alive with the small steamers, row-boats, barges, etc., hurrying to and fro. This, together with crowds of pedestrians and vehicles, passing and repassing, gave us some idea of the lively and bustling city we were in.

How many interesting associations, thought we, are connected with London Bridge, made famous by Dickens and others; and here we recalled to mind an amusing incident that happened on the bridge. An old Irishman who made his living by fiddling for pennies, had laid down his fiddle on the parapet for a few minutes, a sudden gust of wind blew it over, and it was gone. The poor old fellow was telling a pitiful tale of his poverty and loss, when a Quaker came along, and listened. At length he said, "Well, friend, I pity thy case." "Oh, sir, I DON'T CARE A RAP FOR THE CASE IF I HAD THE FIDDLE," said the witty old genius. A general laugh followed, and the Quaker was so amused that he gave the old wit the price of a new instrument.

Our next visit was to the Strand, and up Ludgate Hill; here we were attracted by a great display of gas over a building. The jets spelled the words "Gaiety Theatre," and alongside of it a smaller building had a similar display of jets, spelling the word "Gaiety." This was a drinking saloon gorgeously fitted up, having several of the London "pretty barmaids," whose habiliments were flimsy, gaudy and immodest. They were engaged by their wily masters as "decoy ducks," to attract the soft youths, as we noticed a number of dudes standing at the counter, and being served with liquor and cigars.

There are 50,000 maltsters and 70,000 barmaids in England, and perhaps double that number in the United States and Canada, breaking the Sabbath day in the manufacture and sale of this unnecessary drink. By indulging in your "glass of beer," you "cause a brother (or a sister) to offend." Think of this, and "ABSTAIN from all appearance of evil." Our hotel was "within the sound of Bow-bells," as we ever and anon heard their peculiar sound, reminding us of "Whittington and his cat." "TURN AGAIN, WHITTINGTON, THRICE LORD MAYOR OF LONDON!"

We had letters of introduction to Mr. and Mrs. R. (marriage

connections), who invited us to their hospitable home, where we frequently visited during our stay. As they lived at some distance, we often took the underground railroad, but preferred the top of a 'bus, where we had a full view of the crowded streets, especially at night with their glare of gas lamps. But the most attractive and best lighted buildings were

The Gin Palaces.

Here we noticed a constant stream of common-looking men and women passing in and out. The interior of those "drink-ing hells" are gorgeously fitted up with flashy decorations, consisting of sporting pictures, painted casks, bright pewter measures, drinking glasses and decanters reflected in gilt-framed mirrors, paid musicians discoursing lively airs, and the pretty barmaids, with painted blushes, busy handing out small decoctions of poisonous drinks to a row of bloated-faced bibulists, who were leaning on marble top counters awaiting their turn to be served. Here Satan as an angel of light holds high carnival, through his agents who traffic in human misery. Such was our observation of a London gin palace.

London has been so often and so well described, that it is unnecessary to enter into details of the thousand and one things that are to be seen in that vast metropolis. Suffice it to say, that we visited nearly all the principal places of interest, including St. Paul's Cathedral, the Tower, the Houses of Parliament, Westminster Abbey, the Albert Hall and Memorial, South Kensington and the British Museums, the Bank of England, Trafalgar Square, the National Gallery, the Crystal Palace, etc.

But the most interesting place to the writer was OLD CITY ROAD CHAPEL, the cradle of Methodism. On the wall, in a crescent behind the pulpit, were the cenotaphs of John Wesley, Charles Wesley, John Fletcher, Richard Watson, Adam Clarke, Joseph Benson, Jabez Bunting and others.

We lingered some time reading and pondering over the epitaphs of those once eminent men, who are now in the realms of everlasting joy, and thought of their "works that follow them" in all civilized countries, and howmuch our own fair Canada owes to Methodism, in connection with other Christian denominations who revere the name of Wesley.

Time and space forbid us entering into further details, and here we finish our sketch by quoting, for the amusement of our young friends, the following amusing

LINES ON LONDON.

" Houses, churches mixed together,
'Busses crammed full every weather;
Prisons, palaces contiguous,
Sinners sad, and saints religious;
Gaudy things enough to tempt you,

Outside showy, inside empty;
Baubles, beasts, mechanics, arts,
Coaches, wheelbarrows and carts;
Lawyers, poets, priests, physicians,
Nobles simple, all conditions.
Worth beneath a threadbare cover,
Villiany unmasked, all over;
Women black, fair, red and gray,
Women that can play and pray;
Winsome, ugly, witty still,
Some that will not, some that will.
Many a man without a shilling,
Many a member not unwilling;
Many a bargain, if you strike it,
This is London ! *how do you like it ?* "

CHAPTER V.

LETTERS FROM CANADA AND IRELAND.

THE writer was now tired of sight-seeing, and longed for a little rest, which he enjoyed alone, as his fellow-tourists had left London, G. W. going to Paris, and A. W. to the west of England ; we had, however, arranged to meet in " the Emerald Isle."

After perusing my Canada letters, we proceeded to read a long epistle from our brother G., who, through a pressing business, could not come with us, but followed some weeks afterwards. After speaking of a quick and pleasant passage from New York, he continues, " On the eighth day we sighted Cape Clear, then with peculiar feelings the lines of Sir Walter Scott came to mind :

" ' Breathes there a man with soul so dead,
Who never to himself hath said
This is my own, my native land !'

"The same afternoon we landed in Queenstown harbor. From the deck of our vessel we had an extensive view of this picturesque town, built upon an inclined plane and terraced down to the water's edge. This place was formerly called 'The Cove of Cork,' but had its name changed to Queenstown in honor of Her Majesty's visit to Ireland, and landing here.

" We were now about twelve miles from the city of Cork, and re-embarked on one of the pleasure steamers which ply on the Lee, supposed to be one of the prettiest rivers in the world, with its many windings, sloping lawns, handsome villas, old castles, etc. After passing the nice little towns of Glanmire, Monctown and Black Rock, we had our first view of the tall church spires of Cork, from one of which we heard the chimes of the far famed 'Shandon bells,' which reminded us of the Rev. Father Mahony's celebrated poem, well worthy of a repetition.

" 'THE BELLS OF SHANDON.

" ' With deep affection and recollection
    I often think of those Shandon bells,
  Whose sounds so wild would, in days of childhood,
    Fling round my cradle their magic spells.

" ' On this I ponder where'er I wander,
    And thus grow fonder, sweet Cork, of thee;
  With thy bells of Shandon, that sound so grand on
    The pleasant waters of the River Lee.

" ' I've heard bells chiming full many a clime in,
    Tolling sublime in cathedral shrine ;
  Where at a glib rate brass tongues would vibrate,
    But all their music spoke naught like thine.

" ' For memory dwelling on each proud swelling
    Of thy belfry telling its bold notes free,
  Made the bells of Shandon sound far more grand on
    The pleasant waters of the River Lee.

" ' I've heard bells tolling old Adrian's mole in,
    Their thunder rolling from the Vatican ;
  And cymbals glorious swinging uproarious
    In the gorgeous turrets of Notre Dame.

" ' But thy sounds were sweeter than the dome of Peter
    Flings o'er the Tiber, pealing solemnly ;
  Oh, the bells of Shandon sound more grand on
    The pleasant waters of the River Lee.

" ' There's a bell in Moscow ; while on tower and kiosk O,
    In Saint Sophia the Turkman gets,
  And loud in air calls men to prayer
    From the tapering summits of tall minarets.

" ' Such empty phantom I freely grant them,
    But there's an anthem more dear to me ;
  'Tis the bells of Shandon that sound so grand on
    The pleasant waters of the River Lee.'

"The City of Cork

has a population of about 12,000, is built upon an island formed by the River Lee, which is crossed by nine bridges. The streets are spacious and have good business houses. It has some very fine buildings, and returns two members to the Imperial Parliament. Like every other city it has its excellent* as well as odd characters and wandering minstrels. We were amused, while listening to a ballad singer ; one verse of his ditty we noted:

* Cork is the native place of the Baldwins, Sullivans, McCarthys, Hayes, the Jeffers, the late Adam Miller, and many other well-known names in Canada.—E. M.

    " ' Oh, 'twas in the sweet city of Cork,
        Where Paddy first opened his throttle ;
    He lived at the sign of the fork,
        No wonder he tippled the bottle.
    His mother sold *milk*, they *say*,
        Which made him both funny and frisky,
    And when she put *crame* in his *tay*
        Av *coorse* it was nothing but whiskey.'

Chorus.—" ' Ho ! Ro ! Paddy O'Flannigan,' etc., etc.

" I fear that the Cork citizens use the *crame* freely, as I saw many of them under its influence.

" Blarney Castle and ' The Stone.'

" Blarney is about five miles from Cork. Here we spent a day enjoying the romantic scenery and viewing the old castle, with its massive square tower, 120 feet high, covered with ivy, bearing the date of the fifteenth century, long the residence of the princely race of the McCarthys, Lords of Muskerry and Earls of Cloncarty. But the chief attraction here is 'The Blarney Stone,' which is clasped by two iron bars to a projecting buttress of the castle walls, so that the kissing feat has to be performed by letting a person down headforemost and holding on to his heels—a rather dangerous operation. The author of the ' Shandon Bells ' composed the following lines on the celebrated stone, one verse of which we reproduce :

    " 'A stone is there whoever kisses,
      Oh, he never misses to grow eloquent ;
    Sure he may clamber in a lady's chamber,
    Or become a mimber of the parliment.
    A clever spouter he will turn out, or
      An out and outer—just let him alone,
    Don't hope to hinder him or to bewilder him,
    For he has ' kissed the Blarney stone .

" I will spend a few days here, and then proceed to Killarney; from thence to Nenagh, where I have some business to transact; then to Dublin, where you will find me at the Gresham Hotel.
                          Yours, etc.,   G."

Letter from Our Brother J.

" After spending a pleasant time in our native town, we visited Dublin, Cork, Waterford and the famous

Lakes of Killarney.

"At the latter place we spent two days, visiting the lakes and the romantic scenery around, travelling about thirty miles by various modes of conveyance, such as boats, carriages, and on the backs of lazy ponies, amused with a witty guide and the echoes of gun firing and bugle sounding. But as the lakes have been so often described, we will not enter into particulars, except one incident, that will amuse some of our Canadian friends.

"A's we were passing the Gap of Dunloe, on pony-back, with our feet almost touching the ground, I related an anecdote to the group of tourists who were accompanying us, saying this ride reminds me of the Rev. Lachlan Taylor, D.D., of Canada, who, when visiting the Holy Land, in company with the Hon. Mr. Ferrier, of Montreal, were riding on ponies like ours, when Dr. Taylor's long legs touched the ground. At a certain down grade, the pony made a sudden start and ran from under the Doctor, leaving him high and dry on the hill, shouting after it, 'Stop, you daft beast!' This story caused a laugh, and just as we turned a point who should we see but the veritable Dr. Taylor. Pointing to him, I said, 'and there, gentlemen, is the very man himself; ask him if I am not telling the truth.'

"The Doctor, who knew all our Toronto party, rushed over to greet us, and we had a joyful meeting.

"Our next visit was to Nenagh, our father's native town, where we made a long and delightful visit at the hospitable mansion of C. C. Foley, Esq., who, with his amiable and cultured family, entertained us in a princely style.

"While there we made a pilgrimage to the shrine of 'the Palatines,' a sketch of whose history you gave in your 'Sainty Smith.' As we picnicked under some spreading oaks at Balangar, the native place of Philip Embury and Barbara Heck, we rehearsed their antecedents, and were proud of our descent from such a good old German stock.

"After leaving here we will visit bonny Scotland, England and Wales; and then cross the Channel to Brussels, Paris and the continental cities on the Rhine. Yours, etc., J."

CHAPTER VI.

"COME BACK TO ERIN."

I now bade adieu to London and crossed over to Ireland, landing at Belfast, where I sailed from when a boy. Belfast is one of the finest towns in Ireland, and so much improved that I scarcely recognized it again, especially in the principal streets and the docks. One day, while passing the quay, I noticed a neat little octagon building with a sign-board over it, "The Irish Temperance League, a Cup of Coffee a Penny." "Well done, Belfast!" said the writer, as he stepped into the little building, which was neatly fitted up as a coffee-house. Behind the counter we noticed a young man and a pretty, rosy-cheeked little woman serving out coffee and cake to some sailors and dock hands. How much better, we thought, this than beer or whiskey for working-men. In turn, we sampled the invigorating beverage, and complimented the purveyors by praising the good coffee and neat appearance of the place. The little woman felt flattered and blushed. As I withdrew, I overheard her say to her husband (in a big whisper), "Isn't that the *dacent lookin' man?*"

Londonderry.

My next visit was to the far-famed "Maiden City." To this place we took a circuitous route, passing round the north shore, where we had a delightful view of "old ocean" dashing its white-crested waves against the rock-bound coast. The scenery in this part of Ireland, especially the Giant's Causeway, is grand. As the conductor called out "Londonderry," what a thrill of emotion it sent to our minds. Can this be the far-famed maiden city which withstood an unparalelled siege? Yes, Londonderry in the north, and Limerick in the south, bravely contended for what Ireland now fully enjoys, "freedom to worship God."

Whilst we were meditating on these things our train stopped, and the writer was *besieged* by hotel porters and runners. We looked round for a representative of a temperance house, but failed to discover one.

At length a person solicited our baggage, who wore a high hat with a gilt band, on which was inscribed, .

Canada House.

Our Canadian patriotism was touched, and we said, "Yes, here is my trunk, I will go with you." In reply to our question if any of those omnibusses were his, his answer was, "No, sir, I didn't bring one down with me, but if you'll walk over the long bridge, I will keep my eye on you." As I sauntered towards the city I had a grand view of the old walls, which were surmounted with cannons poking their muzzles in various directions, also of the gates that were closed by the "Apprentice Boys," and various other objects of interest, which brought up many associations.

At length my reverie was disturbed by the sound of wheels rattling over the bridge. I looked back, when lo! and behold! what did I see? "Tell it not in Gath,"—a donkey drawing a little cart with one trunk on it, and a man standing upright with the *gould band* bearing the insignia, "Canada House."

It is said there is only one step between the sublime and the ridiculous, and here it was verified. My first act was a laugh at the sell, then an involuntary "Oh! Canada, my country, what I'm suffering for you!" Yes, we thought how often we have heard of "a one horse hotel," but now it will be most likely outdone by A .ONE ASS TAVERN. As we followed "the low-back car," we consoled ourselves with the thought that the writer was not the first person that was *led by a donkey*. Therefore, our

triumphant entry was not announced by a salvo of artillery
from the old ramparts, but by a roar of the donkey that you
might have heard a mile off.

Our anticipations were realized when the cavalcade stopped
opposite a little one-story house with a sign-board, " Canada
House, *licensed to sell beer, wine and spirituous liquors.*"

We looked inside and saw a man behind the counter with his
coat off, serving out whiskey and beer to a lot of rough-looking
people.

As we stood outside inquiring for one of the best hotels, the
intelligent donkey gave us a look of reproof, and had he the
power of speech like his progenitor of "Balaam" notoriety, he
would most likely have rebuked us in language like the
following:

"So Mr. M., you are too proud to ride with me or stop with
us. You forget when you were a boy in this country, how
delighted you were to jump on a donkey's back; but now you
come back from America, where people ride fast horses and
wear fine clothes, often unpaid for; but let me tell you, Mr. M.,
that greater men than you have rode on donkeys.

"The good book tells how Abraham saddled his ass and rode;
and Jacob's ten sons rode on asses from Canaan to Egypt. The
hard-hearted old prophet, Balaam, when paying a royal visit,
rode upon an ass, and he was the first person who was guilty
of cruelty to animals. Pity Martin's Act was not in force
then; but he was reproved from a higher court. The poor
Shunammite, whose son was miraculously restored to life,
hastened to meet the prophet, riding upon her donkey.

"Judge Jair had thirty sons, who rode on the same number of
asses. Governor Caleb's daughter rode on a donkey, to meet
and consult her father about her approaching nuptials.

"Mrs. Nabal (who afterwards became the queen of good
King David) rode upon a donkey. Saul, the heir-apparent to
a crown, was not ashamed to seek his father's asses, and in the
path of duty, he met the prophet Samuel, who anointed him to
be king.

"But the greatest honor that ever was paid to any animal,
was when the long-expected Heavenly King came meek and
lowly, sitting upon the foal of an ass.

"Therefore, don't despise us, for although we have been
patronized by the rich, we have always been the poor man's
friend. We are called stubborn, but we have good reason to
be so at times, especially when our owners are whiskey drinkers,
who often leave us standing opposite a tavern, shivering with
cold, while our unfeeling and swiping masters are burning their
insides out with what your American Indians call fire-water.

"Now supposing that fellow with the gould band was to
bring me a pail of water and one of whiskey, which do you

suppose I would choose? Why, I would give him a look as much as to say, you must be *the biggest ass* of the two, if you suppose I would drink whiskey instead of water." And the donkey was right.

Having secured larger accommodation, I stopped sqme time here, then bade adieu to the maiden city.

CHAPTER VII.

WARREN POINT AND ROSSTREVOUR.

WARREN POINT is a neat little sea-port town in the county of Down, at the head of Carlingford bay. It is a favorite bathing station, with pure, clear salt water. We visited this place not only for the purpose of its baths, but on account of old associations, as it was here we had our first view of a steamboat, and to this place, from the age of five to ten, we came with our parents to spend the summer months—bathing, fishing and gathering sea-shells on the pebbly beach. Although absent for nearly two score years, every place was familiar; and as we plunged into the incoming tide, the writer thought he was "a boy again."

ROSSTREVOUR,

one of the prettiest watering places in Ireland, is about three miles from Warren's Point, the road leading to it is circuitous, partially covered with shade-trees, with the bay on one side, and the Mourne Mountains on the other, at the base of which there are several handsome villas and a magnificent obelisk on an elevated spot, erected to the memory of General Ross, who fell at the battle of Baltimore, United States, in 1814. This beautiful and picturesque spot is named Rosstrevour, in honor of the brave general.

THE MOURNE MOUNTAINS

are chiefly of granite, covered with foliage. They rise to an elevation of about three thousand feet above the sea level.

We wound our way to the top of Slieve Donard, the highest of the range, where we had a magnificent view of the surroundings. The shipping in the bay, and the houses, appeared like children's toys, and the men like *Lilliputians.* Then, turning round, we saw the mountain peaks in the distance, towering up like sugar-loafs.

CLOUGH MORE, OR THE BIG STONE.

On the apex of the mountain lies a square granite rock about the size of an omnibus. We asked how it came there, and were told the following amusing and ridiculous story:

"You see, sir," said our informant, "that in ould times there was two giants in the neighborhood. The one that lived on this mountain was an Irishman, named *Fin MaCool,* and the other big fellow that lived on the mountain on the other side of the lough was a *Scotchman,* named *Donald MacMurrich,* who was an intruder in this country. So the big fellows quarrelled and began to throw stones at one another, and this is one of the stones that the Scotch fellow threw over at *Fin,* and there it stands; and by the same token, there's the *thrack* of a Scotchman's hand on it, for you know they always take a tight grip of everything." And, sure enough, the impression of a man's hand is to be seen on it to this day.

This big boulder is so nicely poised that you would think an ordinary push would set it rolling ; if so, how slowly it would move at first, but every revolution would increase the velocity, so that it would come down with a rush and destroy the whole town.

So it is with a person commencing to tipple or drink intoxicating liquors : a little at first, then a lilttle more and more, then a rush on the downward grade, and then comes destruction to themselves and others.

A well-balanced sober man, when he climbs to the mountain top, is safe, and can see his way clear.

From the northern brow of the mountain issues an exuberant fountain, which emits about half a foot of water, exceedingly pure. This stream and many others meet in the descent and form a river which, running through a channel of white stone, by ten thousand peaks and windings, make a prospect of waterfalls, cascades, jets, ponds, etc., the most various and delightful.

The lower parts of the mountain are craggy, rude, and covered with hazel, holly, and most luxuriant ferns. Such is a picture of one of the Mourne mountains, where the writer spent most of a summer's day. Our next step was from the sublime to the *ridiculous.* or

A MARKET DAY AT WARREN POINT.

On the following day we attended the fair, or market day, which was held in the town. Every Irishman knows what a market day is in the old land, but for the information of my Canadian readers, we would say that one day in each week was known as " the market day."

On this occasion the little square of the town was crowded with buyers, sellers and loungers. The articles for sale consisted of horses, asses, cows, pigs, sheep, goats, ducks, geese, fowls, farm produce and every description of manufactured articles arranged on standings. Add to this the " Cheap Johns," with auction bells ringing, pedlars and others crying out the goods they have for sale, fakir showmen, tumblers, fiddlers, dancers, ballad singers, squeaking out ditties about "love and murder ; " add to this the squealing of pigs, the bleating of sheep, the neighing of horses, the braying of asses, the bellowing of cows and oxen, the crowing of roosters, and last, but not least, the recruiting parties playing all kinds of popular Irish airs, and you have some idea of a market day in the " *ould sod.*" After examining the wares on the standings, and looking into the canvas tents, where whiskey was being served out to all kinds of people, some of whom were young farmers who had their sweethearts *close to them,* and were coaxing them to drink, perhaps arranging for "a runaway marriage," we sauntered to the horse and cattle market. After a general survey we came to a *garsoon,** who had a nice little donkey for sale. We inquired the price, which he told us in the following words:. "Well, sur, as it's getting late in the day, and I have a long way to go, you may have him for a half a sovereign." "Agreed," said the writer, "if you send him home for me." " Where do you live, sur ? " "About 3,500 miles from here."

On hearing of the distance, he gave a loud laugh, and said, " You must be from America." Then a number of loungers gazed at the writer, and in a little time we were " the centre of a circle," answering as best we could the ridiculous questions about their relations that were living in all parts of Canada and the United States. One man said he had two nieces in the *New Jarsies,* and he would feel obliged if I would keep my eye on them. Another person gave me a slap on the back and said, "Come away and *have a drink.*" He seemed quite disappointed when we declined, by saying, " We are total abstainers." Nevertheless he stuck close to the writer, and was my bodyguard for the remainder of the day. It is needless to say that the little ass was not sent home.

CHAPTER VIII.

DUBLIN.

" Och ! Dublin, sure there is no doubtin',
  Beats every city upon the say ;
'Tis there we've seen O'Connell spoutin',
  And Lady Morgan a makin' tay."

HAVING finished a very pleasant and interesting visit in the north, our next move was to Dublin, the capital of Ireland, where we were to meet our brother G. On our way thither— the fine summer weather gave the country a charming appearance—we were delighted with the beautiful and ever-varying scenery of hill, valley and plain. The closely clipped hawthorn hedges, fencing the fields, of every hue, which formed a natural panorama ; ever and anon little lakes, rivulets, shady

* Between a boy and a man.

groves, old castles, and some of the famed leaning towers came in view.

We were reminded of youthful days on hearing the well-remembered notes of the corncrake, cuckoo, blackbird, thrush, lark, linnet, bull and chaffinch, robin, and a host of other small birds, varied by the magpie and the noisy crows, in the woodlands surrounding the manor houses.

On arriving in Dublin, we drove to the Gresham Hotel, Upper Sackville Street, where we found our brother. I need scarcely to say how pleased we were to see each other.

Dublin, like London and other large cities, has been so often and so well described that we shall not enter into detail, or give a full description of it. However, as it is the capital of our own native isle, we must say something about a place which has such an interesting history. It is truly a beautiful city, closely built, in a neat and regular manner, chiefly of red brick and cut stone. It is about five miles in diameter, and has a population of about 500,000. The River Liffey, which traverses and divides the city, is spanned by seven stone arches and two iron bridges. This river is lined with substantial quays and warehouses, to accommodate the large number of sailing vessels and steamers, which form a wood of shipping.

From the balcony of our hotel we had a splendid view of Sackville Street, one of the finest thoroughfares in the world, literally covered with omnibusses, carriages, jaunting cars and other vehicles, which, together with the smart, quick step of the citizens and moving masses, gives it the appearance of what the Yankee calls "a live city."

In front of our hotel we gazed upon Nelson's monument, a tall fluted column, 120 feet high, exclusive of the statue. The view from the top of this magnificent pillar is grand, as it not only takes in the whole city, but the beautiful surroundings.

After dinner we hired a jaunting-car, and started out for a drive. The first building of note we came to was described by our witty driver as "*the Gineral Post Office*," a very fine structure, supported by six fluted columns, surmounted by three allegorical figures. And just here we were reminded of the oft-told anecdote of an American tourist who, on seeing this building, asked the driver what figures those were on top, and what did they represent. "The twelve apostles, your honour," said the waggish driver. "Why," said the Yankee, "I only see three; where are the other nine?" "Is it the other nine you ax about? why they are inside sortiu' the letthers." Brother Jonathan did not take this in, but on further inquiry he learned that the figures represented Hibernia, Mercury and Fidelity.

Another ridiculous story is told of American tourists who visited here, and were desirous of testing the native wit. In the suburbs they came to a sewer which was being excavated by a number of men, one of whom was in a kneeling position while at work. The spokesman of the party, a foppishly dressed young man, addressed the man thus, "I see, Paddy, you are on your knees." "Yes indeed, sir, an' if you thought as much of your *sowl* as you do of yer body, it's there you'd be, too." "Enough," said the party, laughing at their crestfallen companion, "come away." Passing down Sackville Street, we stopped at Carlisle Bridge, and from that great thoroughfare we had an extended view of the Liffey, shipping, and

THE CUSTOM HOUSE,

one of the finest buildings in the city, with its lofty dome and allegorical figures, representing Britannia and Hibernia in a marine shell, a group of merchantmen approaching, and Neptune driving away Famine and Despair; also the figures of Africa, Asia, Europe and America, together with Navigation, Wealth, Commerce and Industry, and a figure of Hope, sixteen feet high, crowning the whole. The building cost half a million dollars, and took ten years to build it.

THE BANK OF IRELAND, OR OLD PARLIAMENT HOUSE

was our next stopping-place. A large stone building with columns surmounted with the figures of Hibernia, Commerce, Fortitude, Liberty and Justice.

This old building, which has an extraordinary history, is now converted into the National Bank; but still a great part of it remains unaltered, for instance the House of Lords, with its throne, tapestry and furniture is to be seen, as in days of yore. While visiting this chamber and House of Commons, how many associations they brought up, especially of

THE MEMBERS OF THE IRISH PARLIAMENT.

Yes, how often these old walls have echoed to the burning eloquence of Grattan, Curran, Flood, Fitzgibbon, Ponsonby, Molyneux, De Blaquere, Yelverton, St. Boyle, Roche, Heley, Hutchinson, Scott, Connolly, Bowes, Daly, Sir John Parnell, Fitzpatrick, Ogle, and others, many of whom shone as luminaries in the United Parliament at Westminster in after years.

TRINITY COLLEGE

is situated directly opposite the Bank. This grand old structure dates back to A.D. 1311, and passed through many vicissitudes under different sovereigns. It is built of Portland stone and in the Corinthian style. The library is 270 feet in length, and contains over 200,000 volumes, besides many valuable manuscripts.

The apartments are well worthy of a visit, especially the dining-hall, which has life-size pictures of its early students, such as Grattan, Lord Avonmore, Chief Justice Downs, Hussey

Burgh, Henry Flood, Lord Kilwarden, and Frederick, Prince of Wales, the father of George III. In front of the College are bronze statues of Goldsmith and Edmund Burke.

STEPHEN'S GREEN.

After leaving old Trinity we drove to Stephen's Green, a very large square laid out in grass plots. The houses surrounding it are the finest in the city, amongst which are the Royal College of Surgeons, the Museum, the Palace of the Archbishop of Dublin, the Irish Industrial Museum, St. Vincent's Hospital, and last, but not least, the Stephen's Green Methodist Chapel. Within the square, which is surrounded by a beautiful iron fence, are the statues of George II., the Earl of Eglinton, and others.

ST. PATRICK'S CATHEDRAL.

This beautiful cathedral is one of the handsomest buildings in the United Kingdom, lately rebuilt and restored by a brewer, who was knighted by the Queen for this *pious act.* The site on which it stands is said to be the very spot on which St. Patrick baptized his converts. Like Westminster Abbey, it contains many monuments of national statesmen, warriors, poets, divines and armorial bearings of the Knights of St. Patrick.

We attended divine service here in the morning, and at the Stephen's Green Methodist Church in the evening. Our next visit was to

CHRIST CHURCH CATHEDRAL,

also a magnificent structure and a place of great antiquity. It was here the Litany was first read in Ireland.

St. Patrick's having been restored by a brewer, stimulated a rich distiller to perform another *pious act* in rebuilding and beautifying this cathedral. Let us hope that the motives of these manufacturers of intoxicating drinks were more than to appease the Almighty for destroying His good grain, the destruction of which was almost the direct cause of the poverty, disease and crime in the community, and especially in the immediate neighborhood of these churches. Had they built tenement houses for the poor, like the noted Peabody, and employed a city missionary, it would have been an act of restitution and much better than building aristocratic churches, where those poor people never enter.

PHŒNIX PARK.

Our next drive was to this beautiful and extensive park, consisting of about 1,700 acres, nicely varied with grass plots, shrubbery and tall trees, under which tame deer frolicked and might be caressed by visitors. The first prominent object which attracted our notice on entering the park was

THE WELLINGTON TESTIMONIAL,

erected in 1817, by his fellow townsmen of Dublin, to testify their great esteem for him as a military commander. The cost of it was $100,000. The form of it is a quadrangular truncated obelisk. On the front is a likeness of the hero being crowned with laurels, and on the sides are inscribed all the battles of the " Iron Duke."

There are many other places of interest and beauty, such as the Viceregal Lodge, the Zoological Gardens, fish ponds, etc., which we have not space to describe.

On returning from the park we had a full view of

THE FOUR COURTS,

so termed from the courts of Queen's Bench, Chancery, Exchequer and Common Pleas being situated within one building, forming a magnificent pile. A handsome Corinthian portico of six columns occupies the centre, and over it rises a finely proportioned pediment, bearing on its upper angle a colossal statue of Moses.

Kingstown.

There are many other places of interest in the capital which we must omit describing in full, such as the Military Hospital, Constabulary Barracks, City Hall or Royal Exchange, International Exhibition, the Rotunda, National Gallery, Blue-coat School, the Royal Hospital, Botanic Gardens, etc., etc.

Having traversed the city, we then turned our attention to the beautiful surroundings, commencing with Kingstown, a pleasant suburban retreat for the Dublin citizens and tourists. Here they have excellent salt-water bathing, boating, fishing, etc. The numerous villa residences are picturesque and beautiful.

A ROYAL VISIT AND AN IRISH WELCOME.

When George IV. proposed to visit Dublin the inhabitants expected he would come direct to the city, where very great preparations were made to give him a right royal reception, instead of which he landed (incog.) at Kingstown, then a small fishing village called Dunleary, at the mouth of the Liffey, about seven miles from Dublin. The first welcome he got was from an old fisherman, who suspected it was the King from the appearance of the squadron and royal yacht. Curiosity prompted the old native to come down to the beach, and just when the king landed, Paddy held out his hand to him, saying,

" CEAD MILLE FAILTHIA, YORCHE,"

Which in English means " A thousand times welcome, George." The King was so much pleased with the old man's hearty welcome, that he adopted the genuine Irish words as a motto for his carriages, plate, etc. ; hence the origin of "*Cead Mille Fail-thia*," which has gone the rounds of all the English-speaking world. On the very spot where the king landed we saw the monument, with a crown surmounting it, which was placed there to commemorate the landing of royalty. The name of Dunleary was then changed to Kingstown.

CHAPTER IX.

DALKEY AND KILLINEY HILL.

CLOSE to Kingstown, and at the top of the sloping land, we arrived at Killiney Hill, from which place we had a magnificent view of Dublin Bay, second only to the Bay of Naples, which was partially covered with every description of sail, from the pleasure yacht, with its white sails bending in the breeze, to the great man-o'-war, with the Union Jack proudly floating at the mizen top.

BRAY.

The next place of interest was Bray, another fashionable watering place ; population, 4,000 ; twelve miles from Dublin. Tourists from all parts of Britain and other countries visit here, on account of its sea-bathing, and its proximity to the beautiful and romantic scenery of the County Wicklow.

Here we were surrounded by a crowd of jaunting car drivers, who, in a rich Wicklow brogue, accosted us in language like the following : "Do you want to go to de Dargle, yer honor, or to Powerscourt, or de Waterfall, or de Glen of de Downs, or to Delgany, or de Divil's Glen, or de Scalp, or de Seven Churches, or to de Vale of 'Avoca ?'"

We engaged one of the cars and proceeded towards the places above named, skirting the sea-coast, where the white-capped waves of old ocean dashed against the rock-bound coast.

THE GLEN OF THE DOWNS,

is like a deep notch cut out of a mountain, 300 feet below the surface and 1,300 feet below the two "Sugar-loaf moun-tains," so called on account of their conical shape, and which stand like sentinels at the entrance of the Glen. Each side of the sloping rocks are covered with foliage down to the bottom, the aroma of which, together with the sea breeze, gives a delightful sensation. The glen is a mile long. About half way we noticed a number of poor men and women near to a place where clear water was trickling down from the rocks. The group surrounded our car, with tin cups in their hands filled with water, and solicited us to "jist taste the *foinest* water in all Ireland, that sparkles and shines like a kitten's

eye under a bed. *Jist* take a drink, yer honor, and it'll make
you sing in your bed; an no headache, or hair pullin' in the
mornin'." We were overcome by such arguments, and took a
drink. It certainly was the purest, coolest and sweetest water
we ever tasted. After tipping our witty countryman we proceeded to

THE DARGLE,

another glen, where the River Dargle flows, hence the name.
We followed its winding course, and were shown the "*Lovers'
Leap*," and other points of interest, each having a history of
something nonsensical but amusing.

After passing through this romantic glen, we ascended to a
place called

POWERSCOURT.

Here we visited the castle and beautiful grounds of Lord
Powerscourt, and registered our names. At this castle, George
IV. was entertained when he visited Ireland. Four miles from
here we came to

THE WATERFALL.

Here the Dargle joins another river, then the united streams
rush over a perpendicular rock, and the cascades form a beautiful waterfall.

> " Where the glens resound the ca
> Of the lofty waterfall,
> Through the mountain's rocky hall."

Or, in the words of the Psalmist, " Deep calleth unto deep at
the noise of thy waterspouts."

TINNEHINCH

was the next place visited. This beautiful demesne on the
Dargle was purchased by the Irish Parliament and presented
to Henry Grattan, the Irish orator, and is now the property of
of his descendants. Our next stopping-place was

CHARLEVILLE,

another handsome place, the property of Lord Monck, late
Governor-General of Canada. As we proceeded we came to

LUGGALA LODGE,

the property of Mr. Latouch, made famous by one of Moore's
melodies. Here one of the extraordinary Druidical rocking
stones may be seen. George IV. was also entertained here
when in Ireland.

After a circuitous drive over hill and dale the driver called
out, " Now, gentlemen, the next place is called

" THE DEVIL'S GLEN."

Here we entered with peculiar feelings, wondering why it

bore such an awful name; but instead of being dark and dismal (as the name suggested) we found it very much like the beautiful Glen of the Downs, with cascades or waterfalls trickling and rushing from the rocks, 400 feet above us.

GLENDALOCH

was our next and last place on the programme. We found this the most extensive and interesting place of the whole, with its hills, dales and pretty lakes, also piles of ruins, called

"THE SEVEN CHURCHES."

This was said to have been one of the seats of learning in the ninth century, when Ireland was a great luminary, and called "The Island of Saints."

Here we found one of the celebrated "Round Towers," 110 feet high and fifty-one feet in circumference, supposed to have been built by the Druids, 1,400 years ago, and used as an observatory to catch the first glimpse of the rising sun, which they worshipped as an emblem of "the Sun of Righteousness."

We lingered longer here than at any of the other places. Then, very much pleased with our excursion through the Wicklow mountains and glens, we returned to Bray.

THE VALE OF AVOCA AND MEETING OF THE WATERS.

Next morning we took the train for Avoca, twenty-eight miles from Bray. We had old ocean in view nearly all the way, and enjoyed the invigorating sea-breeze. We passed several small towns, but the most prominent was the county town of Wicklow, which is peculiarly situated on a neck of land stretching out into the sea, which gave it a picturesque appearance.

In a little time the conductor called out, "Avoca," there we stopped, and found a number of Jehus with jaunting-cars, and we had to pass through another scene of badgering "Take my car, sur, and I'll show yer honor more of de vale than them other blaggards, who know nothing about it."

At length we selected a car, and entered THE VALE OF AVOCA, called so by having a river of that name, which winds in a lazy, circuitous way through a flat plain, with high hills on each side, similar to the other glens, covered with foliage down to the bottom.

There are very few dwelling-houses in the vale. Such are generally on the banks, amongst which are "Castle Howard" and other mansions, which command a view of the romantic surroundings and old ocean in the distance.

As we proceeded, a small building with two Gothic windows came in view. "What little building is this we are coming to?" was our query to the driver. "That's

"A Swaddlers' Meeting House,"

said the Jehu. We knew that was the nickname for the *Methodists* in Ireland, and sure enough, when we came close, we read the familiar name over the door, "Wesleyan Chapel."

It is said you'll find an Irishman in every part of the world, and often where you least expect to meet one; and so with Methodists and Methodist churches, which are now encircling the globe, numbering at the present time about thirty millions of adherents. But in this secluded place we were surprised to see a modest little chapel.

In a little time we came to a stone bridge, and from it had a view of the two streams, the Avonbeg and Avonmore, which unite and form the River *Avoca*, hence the name

"The Meeting of the Waters."

On a little green island, formed by the junction of the streams, there stands a spreading oak, with a board attached to it, stating that "Under this tree the poet Tom Moore composed his celebrated poem." Here we lunched and drank of the pure waters, then plucked some leaves off the tree, and sang the following verse:

> " There is not in this wide world a valley so sweet
> As the vale in whose bosom the bright waters meet ;
> Oh! the last ray of feeling and life must depart
> Ere the bloom of that valley shall fade from my heart."

Moore, in the above lines, has immortalized this spot. The valley is indeed sweet, and cold must be the heart and dull the head (says a writer), which could pass through it unmoved. This was the finish of our romantic rambles. Next day we returned to Dublin.

There we found letters from Canada, also from our brother J. and his party, who *went* in for an extended tour of England, Scotland and Wales, then crossed to the Continent, where they visited places of note, including Brussels and the field of Waterloo, then to France, Germany, Switzerland, and many places of interest on the Rhine.

CHAPTER X.

MONAGHAN, OUR NATIVE TOWN.

> " The scenes of my childhood once more I behold,
> Where I rambled in youth o'er hill, dale and plain ;
> Absorbed in those young days I eschew being old,
> And dream-like I fancy 'twas boyhood again."

HAVING replied to our letters, we left Dublin, and proceeded to our native town. On our way thither, we passed through

Drogheda, Portadown and Armagh, we were then twelve miles
from our destination, and as we approached the place of our
birth, it was with peculiar feeling, after an absence of about
forty years.

When the conductor called out the familiar name "Monaghan,"
we looked out of the window of our car, but could not distin-
guish any landmark, as the station was built on "made ground
in the plantation," where in boyhood we played under the tall
trees, now removed. However, in a little time we were con-
fronted by a row of eight stone houses in Glasslough Street,
which was built by our father, and bore a date stone,

"MACNAMARA PLACE, 1832."

So called to commemorate Captain Macnamara, late of the Rifle
Brigade, a near relative, who bequeathed a legacy to our sire.

The surroundings now became familiar, the streets and houses
were as we left them, not much changed. The principal differ-
ence was the strange names over the business houses. The new
generation were unknown to us, so that we passed through the
streets of our native town like strangers, gazing at the houses,
and must have appeared so to the natives, who observed our
frequent halts and inquiring looks.

After the evening meal we looked from the balcony of our
hotel on the principal square, called

"THE DIAMOND."

In the centre of which we noticed a change, the old cross surrounded by stone steps (around which so many crowded to
dispose of their wares on market days), was removed, and a
beautiful monument of granite was erected, to commemorate
the late

LORD ROSSMORE.

This, with some new buildings, improved the appearance of the
old Diamond very much.

As we sat in our elevated position during the long evening
twilight gazing at each familiar spot, our reverie was interrupted by the tolling of the bell in the spire of the parish
church, announcing the hour of 9 p.m.; the sound of the church-
going bell brought up old associations, so that the writer and
his brother exclaimed simultaneously,

"JEMMY HUNT'S POT,"

which we called it when boys, as it was then tolled by the
sexton of that name.

Next morning we continued our tour of observation. Passing
down Dublin Street we wended our way to the "Shamble
Square," and here we saw the modest Presbyterian, or Bridge

Meeting-house, which still kept up its reputation for being well filled with an earnest and attentive congregation.

Continuing our walk, we proceeded over the hound hill,* and soon came to a neat cottage surrounded by talls trees, familiarly known in our youthful days as

POPLAR COTTAGE,

then the residence of our grandsire, but now in the possession of strangers, as its former occupants had removed to Upper Canada. We were kindly permitted to walk over the grounds and through the dwelling-house, which brought up many pleasing recollections.

HATCHETTS' LAKE.

Our next visit was to a little oval-shaped lake, in the centre of which was an island covered with tall trees. Around this lake we had spent many happy days—fishing, shooting and swimming to the island.

From there we wended our way to

ROSSMORE PARK.

The picturesque, extensive and beautiful demesne of the Westerna, or Rossmore family, who, although lords of the soil, permitted the inhabitants of the town to visit and enjoy the nicely cultivated and ornamental walks, shrubbery, fish-ponds, flower-beds, etc. Here we were reminded of school-boy days, when

> At Rossmore Park we spent the day gathering nuts and sloes,
> And climbing prickly bushes, regardless of our clothes ;
> Then seeking nests of singing-birds and drinking at the rill ;
> Thus filling up the holidays of 'school upon the hill.'

Returning, we visited the Market Square, which was an interesting part of the town to us, as it was here most of our family were born, there we played at ball, marbles and other games, in the

OLD CUT-STONE MARKET HOUSE,

with its small and large arches, in and around which crowds of farmers and others assembled on the weekly market day. Here the recruiting parties on such days enlivened the throng with the shrill notes and rattling sounds of drums and fifes, while the sergeant *scooped in* the raw recruits through the influence of whiskey and bunkum stories of "martial glory."

In the same square our father's carriage factory and dwelling-house was situated. •There we found a change, the dwelling-house had been divided into two places of business. We asked

* Here we noticed a new brown stone Roman Catholic Cathedral of large dimensions, which, from its elevated position, was an ornament to the town.

permission, and were granted the privilege of inspecting all the premises, which brought up many pleasing associations of youthful days.

Having traversed the principal parts of the town, we hired a jaunting-car, and made an extensive tour around the adjacent country, visiting scenes of our boyhood, including the extensive parks and pleasure grounds of the gentry, also the Kilmore lakes, and other places of interest, where we often heard –

> " The cuckoo's note steal softly through the air,
>   While everything around was most beautiful and fair."

In some places we found peasants who had never been ten miles from where they were born, they had lived in the same little houses their fathers before them had lived in, and would do nothing but what their sires had done.

An amusing story was told us of Mickey Rooney, who lived in a little cabin by a roadside. One day a neighbor was passing, and seeing Mickey in the act of dragging a calf by the tail to the top of the house, which was covered with *scras* (sods), the following conversation took place : " Say, Mickey, what are you doing with the calf ?" "Shure I'm takin' it up to ate the grass." " You goose ; why don't you cut the grass and bring it down to the calf ?" "SHURE I'M DOIN' WHAT MY FATHER BEFORE ME DID." Although the above is a ridiculous story, yet there are more than one Mickey in the world, especially those who drink beer and whiskey, and continue to do so, because their fathers before them drank. Consequently, they are greater geese than Mickey Rooney.

On our return drive we passed Ballyolbany Presbyterian meeting-house, so-called ; close by it lived Bobby Holland, the sexton, whom we had known in our boyhood days. He was a cranky, short-legged little fellow then, and often hurled stones at us from a heap he was breaking, when we mocked him. " I wonder if Bobby's alive," said the writer to his brother. "He is, indeed, sir," said the driver, who had overheard the conversation ; then stopping opposite Bobby's cottage, he pointed with his whip to a little gray-haired man, "There he is, sir." " Why, Bobby," said the writer, "I left you there forty years ago. HAVE YOU GOT THAT HEAP OF STONES BROKEN YET?" "Go lang, ye spalpeen." We all had a good laugh, and Bobby joined in. On Sunday morning we went to the old parish church with Miss Russell, and heard a good sermon from Archdeacon Stark (now bishop).

Around the walls we noticed several marble cenotaphs bearing the names of many of the old inhabitants whom we had known, amongst the rest, one sacred to the memory of RICHARD AND MARGARET JACKSON, who had donated largely to the parish church, also to the Methodist Society, in building them a chapel and endowing the institution referred to in our former pamphlet, "The School upon the Hill."

In the evening we wended our way to the little Jacksonite Methodist Chapel, referred to in a former pamphlet. There we heard a good rousing sermon, which reminded us of the early Methodist preachers, who were workmen that needed not to be ashamed. From the gallery we had a full view of the congregation, at one time well known to us, but now all were strangers; yet every spot in the little preaching-house was familiar and brought up many associations. There was the front bench, on which Mr. Jackson, Sainty Smith and the other leaders sat. In the opposite corner the six widows nestled together, and thus we located and called to remembrance nearly all the worshippers. Where were they now? was our next thought; some had emigrated, others had finished their Christian course, and were now

Where Congregations ne'er break up.

On the following morning we enjoyed a walk of about a mile, to the little farm we once owned. It was, as formerly, surrounded by hawthorn hedges, now in bloom; and while we visited every spot where we spent the sunny hours of childhood, our senses were regaled with the sweet briar and wild flowers, together with a chorus of the little feathered songsters. After taking a last fond look, we bade adieu to our youthful playground, then wended our way to

Milltown and the Blackwater River.

While standing on the stone bridge, and gazing at the old mill with its big black wheel, once covered with the foam of sparkling water, now silent, a melancholy feeling came over us. Involuntarily we exclaimed, "Where are the companions of my youth?" Echo answers, "Where?" Yes, this was the favorite loitering place of

Robert Smith and his blue-eyed Mary.

" With the songsters of the grove,
They told their tale of love,
And sportive garlands wove."

On our way to town, we rested under a shade-tree, opposite a neat ivy-covered cottage close to the roadside. In a little time the front door was opened by a well-dressed, elderly female, who had evidently been a handsome young woman. As she bowed to us we doffed our hats, and asked her the following questions: "Will you kindly inform us what has become of the orchard that was here; and old Molly Flannigan who lived alongside of it, and sold apples to the boys?" She smiled at our questions, and said, "You must have been a long time absent from this neighborhood, as old Molly has been dead about thirty years, and the trees of the orchard were removed about twenty years ago."

We then asked her other questions about the old inhabitants of the town, especially our own family. She was possessed of a good memory, and went into details of all whom we inquired for. But speaking of the family of M., she said, "They emigrated to Canada about forty years ago, and there is not one of them in this country."

At this juncture we smiled, which caused her to scrutinize us, and invite us into the cottage. Scarcely had we entered and removed our headgear, when she exclaimed, "If I'm not greatly mistaken, you are Edward M." I nodded assent, and inquired how she recognized me. "Why, I was a scholar at 'the school upon the hill' when you were there." We inquired her name, and she replied, "At that time it was TILLIE BURTON." "Is it possible you are *Ducky Burton*, the pet name the boys gave you on account of your good looks?" "That's what you mischievous fellows called me. This is a younger brother, I presume; he was not at the school, consequently I never met him."

We then entered into a familiar conversation about the "Sainty Smith" family and the scholars, their history, etc., which was exceedingly interesting to me.

In answer to her inquiries if there were any Monaghan people in Toronto, I replied, "Yes, Tillie, several; and I am happy to inform you that our little town and county has contributed to Canada men who have made their mark in their adopted country. For instance, Governor Aikins, Chief Justice Harrison, Archbishop Lynch, John G. Bowes, who was Mayor of Toronto and Member of Parliament, H. E. Clarke, M.P.P., Rev. John S. Clarke, Robt. Blair, Esq., Rev. W. S. Blackstock, and his son, the eminent Q.C., R. H. Bowes, Q.C., the Messrs. Hanna, Crane, Whitlaw, Dudgeon, Bradshaw, Walker, Russell, Huston, Gregory, McCuaig, Comisky, Scott, Irwin, and several relatives of the writer, many of whom are among the learned professions, leading merchants, government and civic officers, skilled artizans and independent farmers."

"One prominent name you overlooked," said Tillie. "Who?" Sir Charles "Gavin Duffy." "Oh! he emigrated to Australia, our sister colony, and is not one of our Canadian celebrities, nevertheless we are proud to claim him as a native of Monaghan."

"Well," said Tillie, "I'm delighted to hear such a good account of our townsmen in their adopted country; I am prouder of our little town to-day than ever I was before. When you return give them our best wishes, and say that we all 'SHAKE HANDS WITH THEM IN OUR HEARTS.'" The sun of a long summer day was sinking behind the western hills when our interesting conversation came to a close. After presenting her and her family with some little souvenirs, we bade adieu to our intelligent, genial and warm-hearted schoolmate, and wended our way to town.

Then crossing the Gaol Hill, we came to an enclosure containing three stone buildings, which (next to the house we were born in) was the most interesting place in the town to us, no less a place than

"The School Upon the Hill."

We entered through the little iron gate, ascended the steps, opened the door of the boys' room. It was holiday time, consequently vacant. Yet we had no difficulty in locating the desks, forms, Sainty Smith's chair and table, on which rested his Bible, hymn-book and little bell, that announced the opening and closing exercises of praise and prayer; also to stand and make our best bow to the venerable founder when he came to make a visit. On such occasions we let him hear how well we could sing one of Wesley's hymns.

Yes, there sat so-and-so, and this was my seat; here's where Bobby Wright sat, the stupid boy, who afterwards became portrait painter to Queen Victoria. There's the corner where the culprit stood with the dunce's cap on; here's the penitential bench, where we knelt and were whipped for misdemeanors. Then came the mental inquiry, "Where are the scholars of those days?" In various parts of the world you will find them, transplanting the good seed which was sown in their young hearts. Others, like Mr. and Mrs. Jackson, the founders, Sainty Smith, and the congregation in the little chapel, had finished their Christian course and were now among

"The General Assembly and Church of the First-born."

With hallowed memories we bade adieu to this interesting place of so many associations, also to our native town, with the hope of revisiting it at some future day. We then separated, our brother having some business in Dublin and Nenagh, the writer proceeding to Londonderry to meet the Canadian steamer. On arriving at the railway station, we encountered our friend of the Canada House and his intelligent companion, the donkey. For old acquaintance sake, we engaged them to take our baggage to the tender, which conveyed us to Lough Foyle. Here we found the *Sarmation*, and were agreeably surprised to find on board our relatives, A. W. and G. I. W., besides several other Canadian acquaintances.

We had a pleasant passage homeward, and filled up our time rehearsing amusing incidents of travel. As we sailed up the beautiful and majestic St. Lawrence we were proud of the land of our adoption.

We made only a short stay at Quebec and Montreal, and from the latter place we came by lake and river steamer, passing through the far-famed Thousand Islands.

On our first view of Toronto we were reminded of Nelson's beautiful and patriotic poem:

"MY OWN CANADIAN HOME."

"Though other skies·may be as bright,
  And other lands as fair;
Though charms of other climes invite
  My wandering footsteps there;
Yet there is one, the peer of all,
  Beneath bright heaven's dome,
Of thee I sing, O happy land,
  ·My own Canadian home.

"Thy lakes and rivers, as 'the voice
  Of many waters,' raise
To Him who planned their vast extent
  A symphony of praise.
Thy mountain peaks o'erlook the clouds—
  They pierce the azúre skies;
They bid thy sons be strong and true—
  To great achievements rise.

"A noble heritage is ours,
  So grand and fair and free;
A fertile land, where he who toils
  Shall well rewarded be.
And he who joys in nature's charms,
  Exulting, here may view—
Scenes of enchantment strangely fair,
  Sublime in form and hue.

"Shall not the race that tread thy plains,
  Spurn all that would·enslave?
Or they who battle with thy tides
  Shall not that race be brave?
Shall not Niagara's mighty voice
  Inspire to actions high?
'Twere easy such a land to love,
  Or for her glory die.

"And doubt not should a foeman's hand
  Be armed to strike at thee,
Thy trumpet call throughout the land
  Need scarce repeated be!
And bravely, as on Queenston's heights,
  Or as in Lundy's Lane,
Thy sons will battle for their rights
  And freedom's cause maintain.

"Did kindly Heaven afford to me
  The choice where I would dwell,
Fair Canada that choice would be,
  The land I love so well.
I love thy hills and valleys wide,
  Thy waters' flash and foam;
May God in love o'er thee preside,
  My own Canadian home."

So ended our trip to "The Old Sod."

August, 1876.   E. M. M.

THE CITY OF TORONTO.

"My Own Canadian Home."

E. M. M.

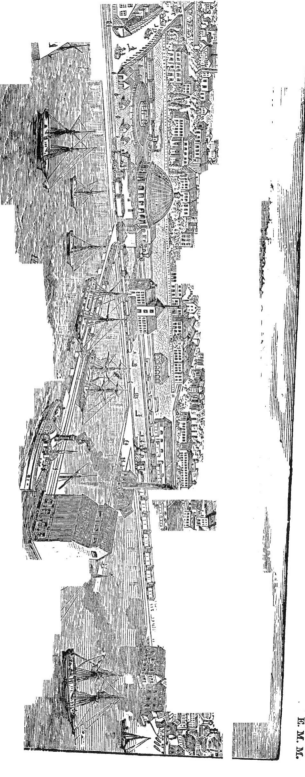

A name derived from town of York, and county of the same;
Once an Indian camping-ground, but now of city's fame,
Whose growth of late, unparalleled, both stimulates and cheers
Our Reverend Worthy President,' and all the York Pioneers.

—E. M. M.

H. Scadding, D.D.

Mammoth House

W E'VE a reputation that is almost national for
LADIES', MAIDS' AND CHILDREN'S MILLINERY
LADIES', MAIDS' AND CHILDREN'S MANTLES
MENS', YOUTHS' AND BOYS' READY-MADE CLOTHING
This spring, and it is being well maintained. Never
before have we had so large an assortment, and
they are, beyond all comparison, brighter and choicer
than those of any other year.

Being *Direct Importers,* we sell all our immense
stock of Staple and Fancy
Dry Goods, Gents' Furnishings, etc., in many in-
stances at less than regular wholesale prices.

In our *Ordered Clothing Dep't* you will find full
lines of English,
French, German and Canadian Cloths. These goods
are unsurpassed for durability and fine finish. First-
class cutters will attend to your orders ; workman-
ship guaranteed. Letter orders promptly attended to.

T. Thompson & Son

136 TO 140 KING STREET EAST
TORONTO

EDWIN A. WHITEHEAD

Architect

OFFICE

S.E. Cor. YONGE AND QUEEN STS.

(Over Imperial Bank)

Entrance No. 1 Queen St. East

TORONTO - - - ONT.

EDGAR & MALONE

Barristers, Solicitors, Notaries,
Conveyancers, &c.

J. D. EDGAR   E. T. MALONE
I. F. EDGAR

Solicitors for the Toronto General Trusts
Company, and
The Toronto Real Estate
Investment Company

OFFICES

GENERAL TRUSTS BUILDINGS
Cor. Yonge and Colborne Sts.

Telephone 372   TORONTO

•Telephone Communication

T. & W. MORPHY

Barristers,

Solicitors, Notaries, Conveyancers, &c.

BRAMPTON, ONT.

THOMAS MORPHY   WALTER S. MORPHY

H. E. MORPHY

Barrister, Solicitor, Notary
Conveyancer, &c.

OVER DOMINION BANK

OSHAWA - - - ONT.

CHAS. W. LENNOX

D.D.S., PHILADELPHIA | L.D.S., TORONTO

Dentist

ROOMS "A AND B," YONGE ST. ARCADE

TORONTO

Telephone 1846

JET AND CRAPE STONE JEWELLERY.

Brooches, 25c., 50c., 75c., $1, $1.50, $2.
Bar Pins, 25c., 50c., 75c., $1, $1 50. $2.
Earrings, 40c., 60c., 75c., $1, $1.50, $2.
Cuff Buttons, 50c., 75c., $1, $1.50.
Bracelets, 50c., 75c., $1, $2.
Ladies' Alberts, 75c., $1, $2, $3.
Ladies' Fobs, 75c., $1, $1.50, $2.

SILVERWARE—BEST QUALITY.

Tea Sets, $30, $35, $40, $50, $60.
Teapots, only $8, $8.50. $9, $10.
Waiters, $4, $6, $9.50, $15, $20, $25.
Dinner Casters, $3, $4, $5, $6, $10.
Cake Baskets, $4, $5, $6, $7, $9 to $12.
Butter Dishes, $2.50, $4, $5, $6.50, $10.
Fruit Dishes, $4, $6, $7, $10, $12.
Pickle Stands, $1, $2, $2.50, $3.50, $5.
Bake Dishes, $12, $15, $18.
Vegetable Dishes, $12, $14, $16, $18.
Salad Bowls, $10, $12, $15.
Biscuit Jars, $3.50, $5, $8, $10.
Ice Pitchers, $10, $12, $15, $18.
Egg Stands with Spoons, $8, $10, $12, $15.
Individual Pepper, Salt and Mustard, 50c., 60c., 80c.
Individual Casters, $2.50, $3, $3.50, $4.50,
Dessert Sets, sugar and cream, $8, $9, $10.
Communion Sets, plated silver, $20 to $25 ; white metal, $10, $12.
Card Receivers, $3.75, $4.50, $6, $7.50.
Sardine Boxes, $5, $5.50, $6, $7, $8, $10.
Syrup Jugs, $6, $7, $8.
Spoon Holders, $4, $5, $7, $9.
Toast Racks, $3, $4, $5.
Combination Sets, $4.50, $5.50, $6.
Call Bells, 75c., $1, $1.50, $2.50, $4.
Vases, $2.50, $3.50, $5, $8, $10.
Toilet Sets, $10, $15, $20.
Nut Bowls, $10 to $15.
Orange Bowls, $9, $12.
Crumb Trays, $4, $8, $10.
Water Sets, $15, $20, $25.
Five o'Clock Tea Sets, $18, $20, $25.
Children's Cups, $1.25, $1.50, $2, $3, $4, $5.
Napkin Rings, 50c., 75c., $1, $1.50, $2.
Knife Rests, 75c., $1.25, $1.50.
Children's Knife, Fork and Spoon, $1.50, $1.75, $2.
Berry Spoons, $1.50 to $3.
Fish Knife and Fork, $5, $6, $7.
Cake Knives, $2.50, $3, $3.50.
Pie Knives, $2.50, $3, $3.50.
Two Nut Crackers, one dozen Picks, in case, $5.50.
Single Nut Crackers, $1 to $1.50 each.

Butter Knives, 75c., $1, $1.50.
Pickle Forks, 75c., $1, $1.55.
Dessert Knives, per doz., $5, $5.50,
Table Knives, per doz., $5, $5.50.
Dessert Forks, per doz., $4.50, $5, $7.
Table Forks, per doz., $5, $6, $9.
Rogers' Carvers, $2.50 to $4 per pair.
Tea Spoons, per doz., $2.50, $4, $5.
Dessert Spoons, per doz., $4.50, $6, $7.50.
Table Spoons, per doz., $5, $6, $9.

FRENCH AND AMERICAN CLOCKS.

Wood and Nickle Cases, Time, 75c., $1, $1.25, $1.50.
Wood and Nickle Cases, Alarm, $1, $1.50, $2.50.
Walnut, Strike, 1 Day, $2.50, $3, $4, $5.
Walnut, Strike, 8 Day, $5, $6.50, $8, $9.
Cuckoo Clocks, $9, $14, $16.
French Marble, 8 Day Time, $11, $12, $15.
French Marble, 15 Day, Strike, $15, $20, $25, $35.
Imitation Marble (Black Wood), Gong Bells, $6 to $12.
Bronze Ornaments and Figures in endless variety.

OPTICAL GOODS.

Gold Spectacles, $4, $5, $5.50, $7, $10.
Gold Eyeglasses, $4, $5.50, $8, $10.
Steel Spectacles, 25c., 50c., $1, $1.50, $2.
Steel Eyeglasses, 25c., 50c., $1, $1.50, $2.
Celluloid Eyeglasses, $1.50, $2.
Reading Glasses, $1, $1.50, $2.
Opera Glasses, $2, $3.50, $5, $8, $10, $12.
Field Glasses, $6, $8, $12.
Telescopes, $1, $2, $3, $5, $8, $10.
Microscopes, $2 to $20.

GOLD PENS AND PENCILS.

Gold Pen and Holder, $2.50, $4, $5, $6.
Gold Pencils, $1.25, $1.50, $2.50, $4.
Gold Tooth Picks, $1.50, $2, $2.50.

WALKING CANES.

Nickle-Headed, $1.50, $1.75, $2, $2.50.
Silver-Headed, $4.75, $6, $7, $9.
Gold-Headed, $8, $10, $12, $15, $20.

FANCY GOODS

In great variety, including 5 o'Clock Tea Sets, Berry Dishes, Epergnes, Toilet Sets, Musical Boxes, Fans, and other articles of virtu, "rich and rare," too numerous to mention, suitable for Wedding and Birthday Presents.

P.S.—Being practical watchmakers, we give special attention to this important part of our business. Our name is engraved on the movements made to order by the best manufacturers in Europe and America; this we do to preserve our reputation of nearly **50 YEARS IN BUSINESS,** as many of the so-called American watches in competition are worthless Swiss imitations. We have only space to give

ONE TESTIMONIAL OUT OF MANY.

"This is to certify that I purchased from Messrs. MORPHY, SON & Co., a Watch with a movement bearing their own name. The first year it varied 1½ minutes, the second it only varied one-half minute from standard time.

"WM. HAWKINS,
"DIXIE P.O."

N.B.—Watches or Jewellery will be sent to any Express or Post Office in Canada, accompanied by a guarantee (and permission to exchange, if not suitable), on receipt of remittance or satisfactory reference.

☞ Special discount to clergymen, churches, or benevolent institutions.

E. M. MORPHY, SON & CO.